VW Beetle

VW Beetle

Paul Wager

CHARTWELL
BOOKS, INC.

Published by
CHARTWELL BOOKS, INC.
A Division of BOOK SALES, INC.
110 Enterprise Avenue
Secaucus, New Jersey 07094

Produced by
Brompton Books Corp.
15 Sherwood Place
Greenwich, CT 06830

ISBN 0-7858-0022-0

Printed in Slovenia

PAGE 1: The 1958 Volkswagen Beetle Cabriolet.

PAGES 2-3: A 1963 VW Beetle in the livery of the Swiss
telephone and postal service.

THESE PAGES: This 1961 car was used by the same owner
for some 32 years, before being offered to a VW
dealership, who now proudly display it in their
showroom, alongside the latest models.

Contents

The Birth of the Beetle

How many readers are aware of the true origins of what is now known and loved throughout the world as the Beetle, Bug, Fusca, Käfer, Coccinelle, Maggiolino or Pulguita; the most successful car in history and even voted the Car of the Century? As they trundle along in a painstakingly restored '56, cruise the streets in a lowered and mean Cal-looker, or tear up the quarter-mile in a fire-breathing dragster, Beetle enthusiasts are driving a car whose origins go right back to the dark rumblings of prewar Nazi Germany.

As most readers will be already aware, the name Volkswagen literally translates to "People's Car," and the Beetle began life in Germany as the product of Hitler's dream to provide a car for the masses of the Third Reich. He wanted a vehicle which the average working-class German family could afford.

In order to fulfil this dream, Hitler enlisted the help of Ferdinand Porsche, an Austrian engineer who had designed his first car by the time he was 21 (the Porsche-Lohner Chaise, powered by hub-mounted electric motors). By the time he had opened his own independent design bureau in 1930, he had already worked for many of the great names in European motoring history, including Austro-Daimler, Mercedes, Daimler-Benz and Steyr, and had been responsible for several landmark designs.

For several years, Porsche had developed a dream of manufacturing a truly affordable small car: as early as 1900, he had designed, developed and constructed a low-cost vehicle, and within a year, he had produced a small four-cylinder, 18bhp car for the Austro-Daimler company. His third small car was also produced by Austro-Daimler, as the four-cylinder, 75kg "Sascha." While at Daimler-Benz, several prototypes (some using the then-unique swing-axle suspension) of his 25bhp "5/25 PS" model were constructed.

Initially, the Porsche design bureau had just two contracts – to design cars for the Wanderer company – and these were terminated only nine months later, when Wanderer merged with Horch, DKW and Audi to become the Auto-Union. The company did then have a few contracts for racing cars, but these were by no means lucrative enough to keep the business afloat, so it would have been in a gloomy atmosphere that Porsche outlined details of the Porsche Project 12 to his staff in 1931: a project which produced many of the features of the Volkswagen.

This was to be a new concept in automobile design. A refined and sophisticated small car, it was to be powered by a lightweight, three-cylinder, radial engine, use fully-independent suspension, and be able to transport four adults in comfort at 100km/h (62mph). Also, the price had to be low enough for the average German family to own it.

In order to keep his design bureau afloat, Porsche attempted to sell the design for Project

12 to the German motor industry. Initially, he was unable to raise interest in the project, but eventually he sold it to Fritz Neumeyer of Zün-dapp, a motorcycle manufacturer seeking to move into the manufacture of small cars. However, mechanical problems involving the engines of the three prototypes (Zündapp had ditched Porsche's suggested four-cylinder horizontally-opposed, air-cooled engine in favor of a five-cylinder, water-cooled radial design, fearing that Porsche's design would be too crude) led Neumeyer to cancel the project, seeing motorcycles as a safer bet in a politically and economically unstable Germany.

However, while working on the Zündapp project, Porsche had been approached by the NSU firm, another motorcycle manufacturer wishing to expand into small-car production, and although this project was cancelled after just three prototypes had been constructed, the car

PREVIOUS PAGES: Ferdinand Porsche at the helm of a racing version of his Lohner-Porsche car, powered by electric motors mounted in the hubs of the front wheels. Porsche himself drove this car in a record-breaking run up the Semering hillclimb, near Vienna.

NSU TYPE 32

Engine	Air-cooled, four cylinder, horizontally-opposed, rear-mounted.
Capacity	1470cc (89.7cu.in.)
Bore/stroke	80mm × 72mm (3.15in. × 2.83in.)
Output	28bhp
Transmission	Four-speed transmission
Suspension type	Torsion bars, rear swing-axles
Top speed	56mph (90km/h)
Tires	5.25-16 or 5.76-16
Track front/rear	1200mm/1200mm (47.2in./47.2in.)
Wheelbase	2600mm (102in.)
Unladen weight	870kg (1918lb)

produced, the Porsche Type 32, bore many similarities to the Beetle. The problems with the Zündapp design had led the Porsche team to abandon the radial engine design in favor of the familiar horizontally-opposed, four-stroke, four-cylinder design, giving 28bhp from 1470cc; and the Porsche designer Karl Rabe had recently patented a space-saving, torsion-bar suspension system which was used in the NSU design.

Despite having been crushed twice, Porsche's designs for a small car were given fresh hope at the opening of the 1933 Berlin Motor Show, where Hitler gave his first speech as leader of the nation and pledged to provide every German family with their own car. He also promised to subsidize entries in foreign events by German racing teams, which was a great boost to Porsche who had already established a separate racing-car department.

It was around this time that Jakob Werlin, a former Mercedes representative and now automobile advisor to Hitler, visited the Porsche offices, and suggested to Porsche that he put his small-car proposal in writing and forward it to the Government Ministry of Transportation. Porsche subsequently met with Hitler to discuss the proposed small car, but Hitler stipulated a price of just one thousand Reichsmarks (Rm) – one-third below the cheapest car then available, and Rm 550 less than even Porsche's original estimated price. At the 1934 Berlin Motor Show, Hitler again related his ideas for a people's car, causing a stir with his promise that if the German motor industry could not build it for the price required, then the government would do so.

On June 22, 1934, the German Automobile Manufacturer's Association (RDA) signed a

LEFT: The man himself – Ferdinand Porsche, the designer behind the Beetle.

BELOW: Porsche and one of the tanks which he designed while head of the Panzer commission.

formal contract with Porsche to develop a people's car; he was to be paid Rm 20,000 to construct three prototypes and deliver them for testing within 10 months. The target price of the car was Rm 900 (later increased to Rm 990), based on a target volume of 50,000 units per year. Despite Porsche's inventive engineering solutions and his previous experience in small-car design, the constant changes that were required in order to meet the target price caused major delays, and the prototypes were not delivered until October 1936.

The agreement stipulated the following technical specifications:

Track	1200mm (47.2in.)
Wheelbase	2500mm (98.4in.)
Max. power	26bhp
Max. engine speed	3500rpm
Unladen weight	650kg (1433lb)
Max. speed	100km/h (62mph)
Climbing capability	30%
Fuel consumption	81/100km (29.4mpg)
Chassis type	Full swing-axle

In constructing the prototypes, a wide range of engines were used, including radial, water-cooled, horizontally-opposed, twin-piston, two-cylinder and three-cylinder designs. The first two cars used a twin-piston, two-cylinder, two-stroke design, which proved unsatisfactory in test-driving, and was later replaced by the four-cylinder, four-stroke, horizontally-opposed engine developed by the Porsche engineer Franz Reimspiess: this engine was to remain unchanged in its basic principles throughout the life of the Beetle. The report of an initial 50,000km test proved sufficiently favorable, and a further 30 prototypes were authorized. These cars would be known as the VW 30 series, and large-scale proving trials were held between October and December of 1936, with the cars covering a total of 2.4 million km, and showing no fundamental problems.

Following the demand for these 30 additional prototypes, the RDA went to Hitler and claimed that the design simply could not be produced for the required price. They offered to rework the design and produce it themselves under a government subsidy. Hitler, however, would not hear of any deviation from Porsche's design, and handed the project over to the German Labor Front (DAF), a government organization, which would produce the cars and sell them directly to the public. Hence, in 1937 the Gesellschaft zur Vorbereitung des Deutschen Volkswagen GmbH ('organization for the development of the German people's car', or "GEZUVOR") was founded.

By the end of 1937, Rm 1.7m had been invested in the project, and work began on a giant showcase factory and town to produce the new car. This was established on the estate of Count Werner von Schulenberg, whose ancestral home was the Wolfsburg castle. Just one year later, the cornerstone ceremony took place, at which

RIGHT: A demonstration run of the VW30 series of prototypes through Berlin in 1939.

BELOW: The three proposed versions of the KdF-Wagen: a Sedan, a Cabrio-Sedan and a full convertible.

Hitler shocked the assembled crowd, by announcing that the car would be known as the "strength through joy" or "Kraft durch Freude" (KdF) car, after the Kraft-durch-Freude organization which had provided Rm 50 million toward the construction of the factory. The announcement caused dismay among those who would be responsible for marketing a car with such a long-winded and pompous name.

Despite delays in the construction of the factory, public support for the KdF-Wagen continued, with the announcement of a savings plan (which differed from conventional hire-purchase agreements in that the car was not delivered until all payments had been made), by which prospective customers could pay five Reichsmarks a week to the Labour Front, and once they had saved the necessary 990 Reichsmarks, could collect their new car from the factory. Extremely harsh conditions were attached to the scheme, and to miss a single payment would result in the whole agreement becoming void. Saving the purchase price would of course take four years, although additional payments could be made for earlier collection, and the scheme was also extended to children, who could save five Reichsmarks per month.

However, with the outbreak of war, not one of the savers ever received their car, although contrary to popular rumor, the plan was not a deliberate fraud in order to raise money for war preparations. The money (336,668 Germans had joined the scheme, providing Rm 110m by 1938) was held in a Berlin bank account, and sequestered by the Russians after the war. Following a court case begun in 1950 against Volkswagen by disgruntled KdF savers, a settlement was eventually reached in 1961, with the company offering DM 100 in cash compensation, or a DM 600 discount on the price of a new Beetle: some 20 percent of them chose the car.

The KdF-Wagen was displayed for the first

VW 30 PROTOTYPES

Engine	Air-cooled, four cylinder, horizontally-opposed
Capacity	900cc (54.9cu.in.)
Bore/stroke	70mm × 64mm (2.76in. × 2.52in.)
Output	22bhp
Transmission	Four-speed transmission
Suspension type	Torsion bars, rear swing-axles
Brakes	Single-circuit, cable, four drums
Top speed	62mph (100km/h)
Tires	4.50-17 or 4.50-16
Track front/rear	1250mm/1250mm (49.2in./49.2in.)
Wheelbase	2400mm (94.5in.)
Unladen weight	650kg (1433lb)

KÜBELWAGEN TYPE 82

Engine	Air-cooled, four cylinder, horizontally-opposed, rear-mounted. Solex 26 FV1 carburetor.
Capacity	985cc (60.1cu.in.)
Bore/stroke	70mm × 64mm (2.76in × 2.52in.)
Output	24bhp
Transmission	Four-speed transmission, limited-slip differential, rear-wheel drive.
Suspension type	Torsion bars, rear swing-axles
Brakes	Single-circuit, cable, four drums
Top speed	50mph (80km/h)
Tires	5.25-16 or 200-12 Tropical Eqpt.
Track front/rear	1356mm/1360mm (53.4in./53.5in.)
Wheelbase	2400mm (94.5in.)
Unladen weight	750kg (1653lb)

LEFT: The Type 82 Kübelwagen used only rear-wheel drive, but was fitted with a limited-slip differential to give it incredibly good cross-country performance.

RIGHT: The dashboard of the Kübelwagen was minimalist to say the least!

BELOW: The rudimentary dashboard of the Type 166 Schwimmwagen, showing the gearshift layout which included four-wheel drive and an extra-low cross-country gear.

time at the Berlin Automobile Show in 1939, and it was at this show that a Dutchman, Ben Pon, met with Hitler and subsequently gained the official distributorship for the car in the Netherlands. It was also Ben Pon who would later make the first rough sketches which would lead to the design and production of the Volkswagen Type 2 van.

With the outbreak of World War II, Hitler reluctantly agreed to cancel all civilian projects which could not be completed during 1939, and this of course included his KdF-Wagen. Work on the factory ceased, but public enthusiasm for the car was unabated. In fact, it was not until August of that year that Robert Ley announced the KdF saving scheme.

Despite postwar suggestions that the plant had been designed all along as an armaments factory, it was not requisitioned by the Reich Air Ministry until just before KdF-Wagen production could begin, and the management even had to hunt around for jobs, in order to keep the plant afloat. One of their largest contracts during the war was the construction of millions of sheet metal army stoves destined for the Russian front, and although much of the expensive machinery

and production equipment ordered from America had never actually arrived in Wolfsburg (owing to the American trade embargo), the plant was still able to produce engines, which were used as military generators.

Seeing that their dream was on the brink of disappearing in the wartime confusion, Ferdinand Porsche and his son Ferry decided to adapt the KdF-Wagen for wartime use, in order to keep their design alive. The result of this was the Kübelwagen, a literal translation of which is "Bucket Car." By adding reduction gears to the rear axles, the car could be driven at a soldier's walking pace, and gained extra ground clearance for off-road use; a limited-slip differential was used to compensate for the lack of four-wheel drive, and its cross-country capability was highly regarded.

Porsche however had to struggle against red tape to obtain a military order for the Kübelwagen. Only after a harsh test against the "jeep" designed by the military supply office, and by going direct to Hitler to convince him that the car was a sound design, was an order eventually received for an initial 400 Kübelwagens. These were assembled in Wolfsburg using bodies constructed by Ambi-Budd Presswerk in Berlin. However, the attitude of the supply office suddenly changed, no doubt influenced by Hitler's decision to attack the Soviet Union, and in December 1940, the 1000th Kübelwagen rolled off the production line.

Several variations on the Kübelwagen theme were also produced, including personnel, radio and siren vehicles. More esoteric versions included the Type 155, which was a Kübelwagen using half-tracks, a mock-up of a tank to use as a decoy, and the Type 157, which was equipped with flanged wheels for running on railway tracks. In fact, the performance of the Kübelwagen was so good that Allied personnel often kept and used captured examples, encouraging

the U.S. War Department to issue a handbook in 1944, entitled *The German Jeep*, to help U.S. personnel drive and maintain the unconventional vehicle.

The Kübelwagen may have been good in battle on dry land, but the one thing it couldn't do was float: enter the Type 128, or Schwimmwagen as it's more popularly known. In 1940, Porsche was engaged by the Army Office of Armaments to build an amphibious vehicle for the Heerespioniere [Pioneer Corps], and the result was the Type 128, a cross-country and amphibious vehicle using four-wheel drive and an extra-low cross-country gear. To increase ground clearance, Kübelwagen-style reduction gearing was used at the rear, and special stub-axles drilled to take driveshafts were used at the front. The body was constructed of welded steel, with rubber seals in all the crucial openings. When on the water, the wheels kept turning, and were still used for steering the vehicle – with a dashboard indicator showing the driver their position – but propulsion was provided by a rear-mounted propeller which could be swung down into position to engage with a shaft driven from the crankshaft.

The additional standard equipment with the Type 128 included measuring poles for checking the depth of the water, a shovel, and paddles for emergency use, or when silent progress was necessary. Around 30 of the Type 128 were produced, before it was subsequently refined into

LEFT AND BELOW: The Type 166 Schwimmwagen – This particular example has been "butchered" by a postwar owner to insert a door – proper Schwimmwagens did not have any doors.

RIGHT: This picture shows the extensive bomb damage suffered by Volkswagen's body-building plant.

the smaller Type 166, at the request of the SS. This vehicle had virtually unlimited cross-country capabilities, and some 14,283 were produced beween 1942 and 1944 before shortage of materials eventually halted production; it has been estimated that around 150 of the vehicles survive today.

Several military versions of the KdF sedan were produced, beginning with the Type 82E, which was based on the KdF-Wagen, but with a stripped-down military interior and using the Kübel chassis. The Type 87, built only in small numbers, was a four-wheel drive version of the KdF-Wagen, fitted with a roller at the front to help clear large obstacles, and generally known as the Kommandeurwagen. It was mostly used by Rommel's Afrika Korps, and the design sketches for the Type 87 formed the basis of the design for the amphibious vehicles. Some Type 87s were fitted with tropical equipment which included balloon-style Kronprinz sand tyres which entailed a specially modified front axle, and despite the generally spartan equipment, most of the Kommandeurwagens came equipped with a large fabric sunroof.

In addition to the various military variants, some 630 non-military KdF-Wagens were constructed during the war; not surprisingly they were not delivered to expectant KdF-savers, but to the privileged Party officials as staff cars. As the war dragged on, fuel became even more scarce, and many vehicles were converted to use gas generators, burning anthracite, coal, coke or even peat, as were a number of Kübelwagens and Type 82 cars, which were fitted with Porsche-designed gas generators.

The plant was also used during the war for air-plane repairs, and to construct the fuselage and wings of the V-1 flying bomb, but it escaped serious bombing until the end of the war, when the Allies attempted to stop the source of the V-1 bombs. However, by 1945, around one-third of the plant was unusable, with the press-shop badly damaged, and the cost of repairs was estimated at Rm 156 million. In March 1945, Hitler made a desperate visit to the eastern front to encourage his troops, driven by his chauffeur in a Volkswagen. Ironically, it was the last car journey of his life.

SCHWIMMWAGEN TYPE 166

Engine	Air-cooled, four cylinder, horizontally-opposed, rear-mounted. Solex 26 FV1 carburetor.
Capacity	1131cc (69cu.in.)
Bore/stroke	75mm × 64mm (2.95in. × 2.52in.)
Output	25bhp
Transmission	Four-speed transmission plus cross-country gear, four-wheel drive, propeller drive by chain and shaft from crankshaft.
Suspension type	Torsion bars, rear swing-axles
Brakes	Single-circuit, cable, four drums
Top speed	50mph (land), 6mph (water)
Tires	5.25-16, 690-200 or 200-12
Track front/rear	1220mm/1230mm (48.0in./48.4in.)
Wheelbase	2000mm (78.7in.)
Unladen weight	910kg (2006lb)

Rebirth and Recovery

The town of KdF-Stadt fell within the British zone of occupation, and when the Occupation forces learned of the large amount of labor available in the town, a detachment of REME officers was posted to the plant, to organize a repair workshop for captured enemy vehicles. The town was suddenly a busy place again, and became one of the more comfortable of the occupied towns, with a population of 17,109, of which some 9,000 were employed in the factory. It was renamed Wolfsburg in May 1945, after Count von Schulenberg of Wolfsburg who had given up his land for the factory.

While the main postwar occupation was rebuilding damaged vehicles, a dozen or so Kübelwagen bodyshells were found among the debris, and these were used to construct some complete vehicles, using spare parts and components from damaged cars. In the immediate aftermath of the war, the British were anxious to construct some barrier against the Soviets by reviving the country's industry, and also to provide transportation for the country. So in August 1945, a certain Major Ivan Hirst, later assisted on the administration side by Alistair McInnes, was sent to Wolfsburg by the Control Commission for Germany, with express orders to get a Volkswagen – either the Kübelwagen or sedan – into production. A war-damaged car was refurbished and sent to Army headquarters, which resulted in an order for more vehicles, and 20 million marks were advanced as working capital.

Since it had not been in operation before the war, the factory was officially classed as a war plant, and so was on the list of facilities which could be dismantled, with the machinery going to the Allies as war reparations. The American forces were opposed to the factory, regarding it as an industrial operation not needed under their Morgenthau Plan: formulated in 1944, the Morgenthau Plan aimed to reconstruct Germany as an agriculture-based economy, and although it was modified in 1946 to permit certain industries without military potential, it would have put the German economy back to 1936 levels. The factory's future was also threatened by the Soviets, who were anxious to receive reparations as soon as possible.

However, as it was providing essential transportation for the authorities running the zone of occupation, a four-year stay of the dismantling order for the Wolfsburg plant was obtained. Under the reparations orders, no major repairs could be made to the factory, but production was able to begin, albeit in dreadful conditions and with crippling materials shortages. By the end of 1945, 58 new cars had been constructed from the parts available.

In 1946 the factory again came under threat; if production could not be increased to 1000 units

PREVIOUS PAGES: Ivan Hirst (left) with an early postwar production Beetle.

RIGHT AND BELOW RIGHT: Two views of the factory at Wolfsburg immediately after the war. The bottom picture shows the factory's southern frontage, with the power plant in the background. A Volkswagen sedan of the time can be seen on the extreme left, alongside two German army Kübelwagens.

BELOW: The final assembly line, as it appeared during immediate postwar production under British control.

ABOVE: An early prototype of the two-seater convertible.

LEFT: With its under-stressed, low-revving engine and high gearing, the Beetle was designed from the beginning with the Autobahn in mind.

per month, the factory would be deemed too expensive to operate, and would be dismantled. Ivan Hirst enlisted Richard Berryman, a former RAF officer, who had gained mass production experience working for General Motors before the war. He explained to the workers that it was in their own interests to increase production, and provided more basic essentials such as food and blankets; productivity was improved and the plant just escaped dismantling, producing 1003 vehicles in March 1946 and a total of 10,020 cars during the year.

Due to the postwar territorial changes, Germany was now much more dependent on food imports (50% of its food being imported compared to just 20% before the war), and food shortages were common as farmers struggled to attain prewar production levels. It soon became apparent to the management at the factory that significant increases in production could be obtained simply by adding meat to the workers' lunchtime soup.

Production continued in this manner, with supplies and components being obtained by subterfuge, or by barter in exchange for cars. When the supply of carburetors dried up, they made their own housings, with the precision components being manufactured by a local camera manufacturer. As cars were produced, they were sold under a list of priorities, with the top priority being the British Occupation forces, followed by the police, fire services and local government.

In 1946, Ben Pon made a second visit to the factory and procured a second contract to sell the Volkswagen in Holland, taking five cars back in 1947. This historic transaction marked the rebirth of Germany as an exporting nation, and by 1952, Pon would be taking delivery of his 10,000th Volkswagen. Several others were seeking export licenses, and within Germany, many applications for dealerships were being received,

yet production levels could not be increased. By now, most of the British staff had left, and a strong German management team had been established. Colonel Charles Radclyffe, the man responsible for the motor industry in the occupation zone, and the man who had initially sent Hirst to the factory, decided it was time to look around for a German production executive to take full charge of the factory, and guide it through Germany's economic revival.

He eventually found his man in Heinz Nordhoff, a former Opel executive, who had been the company's representative on the RDA panel during the prototype days of the Volkswagen, and who had been hoping to return to General Motors employment after the war. However, his role in managing a truck plant during the war meant that he was prohibited from holding a managerial position in the American sector, in which the only General Motors plant in the country had ended up. Initially reluctant to take over the Volkswagen plant, he eventually took the post of Generaldirektor in January 1948, after learning that he would be unlikely to find employment with the American manufacturer. Initially unimpressed with the Volkswagen, he is quoted as saying that "The car had more faults than a dog has fleas," but under his leadership, improvements in construction quality and design were gradually achieved, making the Beetle one of the best-quality cars in its class.

Nordhoff's arrival coincided with the decision to return the Volkswagen company to German control: Order No. 202 from the occupying forces transferred the rights to the factory to the Federal Government in Bonn, who in turn appointed the province of Lower Saxony to manage their interests. In 1947 Porsche was released from French custody and when being driven home through Germany, was astounded to discover that six in every 10 cars on the road were Volkswagens.

Using his mass-production experience from his time at General Motors, Nordhoff's first actions were to organize repairs to the damaged factory, and to increase production. A production quota of 22,000 vehicles was allocated to Volkswagen in 1948, but to reach this target, additional machinery and materials would be required – and this could only be achieved by increased sales, so the plant was trapped in a vicious circle. An increase in output was necessary to ensure the financial stability of the plant since at the current production level, the car was costing more to produce than its selling price – which had been set by the British occupation authorities without any attention to production costs. Cars could only be sold to the occupying forces at Rm 5000, but the car actually cost just over Rm 5000 to produce.

A handful of dealers were selling the cars in Germany, and Ben Pon in Holland and d'Ieteren Frères in Belgium were taking some exports but

LEFT: The two-spoke steering wheel, chrome dashboard trim, and ivory-colored control knobs were introduced in 1949, while the ashtray above the starter button came along in 1950. This 1951 car was the last model to receive this style of dashboard, as a new design was introduced in 1952.

BELOW LEFT: This 1951 model split-window Beetle features the ventilation flaps in the front quarter panels, which were used for this year only.

RIGHT: The interior of this split-window Beetle shows the increased luggage area when the rear seat was folded down. The metal rails to protect the carpet were introduced in 1949.

the cars were still proving difficult to sell abroad as anti-Nazi feelings lingered, and the necessary volume was still not being reached.

However, in June 1948 the fortunes of the plant suddenly changed, with what Nordhoff later referred to as "the single most important act in Volkswagen's climb to success." This miracle took the form of a currency reform, when the long-devalued Reichsmark was replaced with a new currency, the Deutschemark, at a rate of 15 to 1 – a shock to the German public who had been expecting a rate of 3 to 1 or even 2 to 1. Each citizen initially received 40 Deutschemarks to cover the first week's living expenses, but in a country with little faith in paper money, most of this was spent almost immediately, and traders and shopkeepers throughout the country were soon anxious to exchange the massive amounts of new money they took in this initial spending spree, for transport.

A sudden upturn in orders was the result at Wolfsburg, and fortunately, Volkswagen were able to capitalize on this as slow sales had caused a stockpile of cars to build up in the factory basement – resulting later in allegations that Nordhoff had been warned in advance of the planned currency reform. German industrial production of all kinds increased by 50 percent in the year following the currency reform, and Volkswagen received its first foreign-currency income in 1948, amounting to some 21 million Deutschemarks.

Of course the currency reform also caused a few headaches at Volkswagen; the company's cash reserves had been devalued by the reform to just Dm 62,000, and the workforce's wages were some Dm 400,000; in order to pay his workers, Nordhoff had to ask his dealers to bring to the factory all the cash they had taken in the previous weeks from the sales of cars. Such had been the demand for the cars that the wages were covered. By 1949, deliveries of completely knocked-down (CKD) cars began, for assembly in Ireland and Brazil, and with the reconstruction of the factory complete, the Volkswagenwerk finally had the same floor space as before the war.

By 1950, there was a waiting list for the car, but despite improvements under Nordhoff's leadership, production was nowhere near the 22,000 cars authorized under the 1948 quota, and he was only too aware that in order to increase production, an increase in capacity would be required. The Beetle bodyshell was very expensive to mass-produce, due to its complex shape, and equally complex tooling was needed to produce the cars efficiently. This of course would require U.S. dollars, which could only be gained from American exports. The U.S. was one area which Volkswagen had not explored so far: Ben Pon had first taken a car to America, to research the market, in 1949, but met with little interest and even had to sell the car to pay for his ticket back to Holland!

Until 1953, the car was sold through Max Hoffman, an imported-car specialist in New York, but the approach used proved unsuccessful. By attempting to sell the Beetle to the customers of expensive European sportscars, he could only achieve a pitifully low volume of sales – a situation not helped by Hoffman selling only the Standard version, not the more luxuriously-appointed Export Beetle. It was not until Nordhoff sent a hundred or so Volkswagen personnel to the U.S. to form a proper Volkswagen export department, that sales began to increase, rising to 6343 in the first year. The U.S. organization continued to grow, providing much-needed service and technical backup with the arrival of 26 service engineers in 1952, and by 1955, Volkswagen found itself at the top of the imported-car sales table, with 28,097 Beetles sold in the U.S. in that year. Central to the firm's success in the American market was Nordhoff's insistence on providing a comprehensive servicing and spares backup, with a fleet of factory-trained mechanics deployed to educate the dealers in servicing the unconventional vehicle. By the 1960s, Volkswagen were proudly boasting in their advertising that with every one car imported, they imported enough spare parts to rebuild it.

In 1959, a new head of the American opera-tions was appointed – Carl Hahn. Quick to adopt American marketing techniques, he made the now famous decision to begin advertising the car. While demand still exceeded supply, Hahn was conscious of the fact that opposition was planned from the big American manufacturers who had small cars of their own waiting in the wings, and he decided to preempt any effect of this on sales of the Beetle. After an extensive search for an advertising agency suited to selling the Beetle in the right way, Hahn eventually settled on Doyle Dane Bernbach Inc. (DDB), an agency well-known for its creative style, which had previously worked on campaigns for El-Al and Polaroid.

The partnership between Volkswagen and DDB was to produce a series of adverts that are now regarded as classics, and which were quite unique at the time. Intelligent and self-deprecat-ing, they pioneered an "honest" style of advertis-ing, selling the car on its virtues of dependability, quality and non-obsolescence in an age when automobile advertising, especially in the U.S. was glamorized and fanciful, and each new year's model was longer, lower and wider. Many of the ads actually made use of the fact that the Beetle was the same from year to year, as a result of Nordhoff's policy of updating the design only

ABOVE AND ABOVE RIGHT: The Standard model sedan was extremely spartan, down to its painted bumpers and externally-mounted horn: this is a 1949 example.

RIGHT: This rare 1950 model Beetle with the optional fabric sunroof was one of only 324 Beetles sold in the U.S. that year. During its long life it has acquired just a few period accessories!

when worthwhile technical improvements could be incorporated. This was in stark contrast to the built-in obsolescence of most American models of the 1960s.

Of course, it didn't really matter if the DDB ads sold more cars or not: demand kept on coming anyway. In 1963, more Beetles were sold in the U.S. than in Germany, and construction began in March 1964 on a new plant at Emden, initially solely to supply the North American market. However, the successful advertising campaigns had certainly made Volkswagen a household name. The 500,000th Volkswagen reached the U.S. in 1960, and between 1960 and 1968, Volkswagen sales in the U.S. climbed steadily to a peak of 423,000 in 1968. It was all a far cry from Max Hoffman's claim back in 1950 that a maximum of only 2000 cars a year could be achieved.

Carl Hahn, the man responsible for initiating the advertising campaigns and the force behind much of the Beetle's success in the U.S., went on to become Chairman of Volkswagenwerk AG from 1982 until 1993, by which time the firm was boldly claiming to be Europe's largest car maker, having swallowed up Audi NSU Auto Union GmbH in the 1960s, and then IFA (Trabant) in the former East Germany, SEAT in Spain and Skoda in Czechoslovakia by the early 1990s.

From Splits
to Squares

With the 1953 model year, the two small rear windows "Pretzelfenster" were changed to a single oval window, and these 1953-1957 cars are referred to by enthusiasts today simply as "oval window" cars, or "Ovals," with their pre-1953 counterparts known correspondingly as "split-window" cars or "Splits." In 1954, the engine capacity was increased from 1131cc to 1192cc, raising output from 25 to 30bhp, and top speed to 68mph, and the following year twin exhaust tailpipes were fitted. This gradual evolution co-incided with ever-increasing sales, and in February 1956, the 500,000th export Volkswagen left the Wolfsburg factory, destined for Stockholm.

The original KdF model range had been drawn up to include a sedan, a sunroof sedan or "cabrio sedan," and a full convertible. Although both four-seater and two-seater convertible prototypes had been constructed under Hirst's leadership, Volkswagen eventually went to outside suppliers to construct their convertible models, approaching Karmann of Osnabrück, and Hebmüller of Wülfrath, both long-established coachbuilders. Karmann engineers visited the factory in 1946, but were unable to conquer the rigidity problems introduced by slicing off the roof until 1949, when their interpretation of the Volkswagen convertible went into production, becoming the only officially-sanctioned convertible model, and one which was destined to keep rolling down the Osnabrück production line until

1979. The association between Karmann and Volkswagen continued into the 1990s, with the construction of the Golf Cabriolet, the Scirocco and the Corrado all being entrusted to the firm.

The Hebmüller version of the Beetle convertible was a stylish 2+2 design, with a long rear deck and a soft-top which disappeared from sight when lowered. The first three Hebmüller cars were produced in 1948, and following VW approval, some 680 cars were constructed before a fire devastated the Hebmüller works in 1949, bankrupting the poorly-insured company. The remaining cars were finished by Karmann, and in total, 696 examples of the Hebmüller model were produced; it is estimated that some 50 or so are still in existence in various stages of restoration, making this the rarest production Beetle convertible model.

Several other coachbuilt interpretations were constructed on Beetle chassis during the 1950s, although the launch of Volkswagen's own coachbuilt car, the Karmann Ghia, in 1955 in coupé form, and in 1957 as a convertible, increased VW's official opposition to independent builders. The company's refusal to supply rolling chassis to customers drove many such firms to purchase complete cars and simply discard the body, although the idea of scrapping a new 1950s Beetle bodyshell would raise a few eyebrows today.

One of the first of these was Wolfgang Denzel, who had begun by building a "special" on a Kübelwagen chassis, and by the mid-1950s was

PREVIOUS PAGES: This beautiful 1961 Beetle has the 34bhp engine which was introduced for the 1960 model year.

BELOW, RIGHT AND FAR RIGHT: This 1955 oval-window car features the optional fabric sunroof. The rear lights were changed in 1955, discontinuing the separate brake light lens on top of the lamp housing.

BELOW RIGHT: As the license plate suggests, this is a 1949 example of the Hebmüller two-seater convertible. The Hebmüller was, of course, never sold in North America – this Californian-registered car was imported to the U.S. from Germany in 1971.

squeezing 65bhp and 93lb ft of torque from a 1281cc engine using twin Solex 40 P II carburetors. By making his "Denzel 1300," optionally available with aluminum bodywork, a top speed in excess of 100mph was attainable.

The Swiss-built Enzmann 506 used an Okrasa TSV-1300/34 engine conversion in a two-seater bodyshell, to give the 10cwt car a top speed of over 100mph and an acceleration of 0-60mph in just 12 seconds; while the Colani GT designed by industrial designer Luigi Colani, was one of the less attractive body styles to grace the VW chassis, and was sold through a mail-order house.

Between 1950 and 1956, the Römetsch-Karosserie company of Berlin produced their "Beeskow" model, named after its designer Johannes Beeskow. These cars were hand-built in a traditional manner, using an aluminum body on a steel and wood frame, each car taking around 1000 hours to finish. Some 500 examples of the Beeskow were sold, many finding their way to society's élite – customers included the King of Sweden. The car featured front-opening "suicide" doors, and a single rear seat which was installed sideways in order to increase rear legroom, with a small luggage area behind it. The Beeskow was succeeded by the "Sport-Kabriolett" model, also available as a coupé, in 1957. This all-new model featured a new body, reminiscent of American designs, and used a twinport, dual carburetor Okrasa engine conversion.

The firm also produced a four-door taxi from 1951, again designed by Johannes Beeskow, and using a Beetle bodyshell and chassis lengthened by some 8⅔in. (22cm). The roof was cut behind the original doors, and a new panel inserted, with new rear door pillars supporting the roof. The rear quarter panels were shortened, along with the original doors, to allow for larger rear doors to be used, and the entire conversion cost around DM 2000.

The Römetsch Sport-Kabriolett was produced until 1961, when the rising production costs of these labor-intensive cars and the East-West divide of Berlin sharply halted their production: most of the Römetsch staff lived in the Eastern sector and could not get to work at the factory in the western sector.

The Drews "Sport Cabrio" was coachbuilt in aluminum and is now one of the rarest of the coachbuilt cars, while Dannenhauer & Stauss of

ABOVE AND ABOVE RIGHT: This 1957 Cabriolet took some three and a half years to restore, and features a leather-trimmed interior – a factory option back then.

BELOW LEFT: Volkswagen lacked the ornate embellishments of contemporary American cars, and this stylized "Volkswagen" script was a popular dealer addition in the 1960s. The enamel Wolfsburg crest was changed in 1959 to a less colorful design.

RIGHT: A 1958 example of the Römetsch Sport-Kabriolett, first introduced in 1957, with a specification including a twin-port, dual-carburetor Okrasa engine conversion. With the division of Berlin, production of these aluminum-bodied cars ended in 1961.

OVERLEAF: This painstakingly-restored 1955 Beetle is powered by a 1500 engine, complete with 12V electrical system. The transformation from a £165 ($240) hulk included four new wings, two rear-quarter panels, the front valance, and spare-wheel well! The sunvisor above the windshield was popular at the time.

Stuttgart, produced a model which was similar in appearance to the Porsche models of the time. Beutler of Thun, the firm which had produced the first bodies for Porsche's 356, built a 2+2 coupé, a Beetle-based station wagon, and a delivery van. Using as much standard bodywork as possible, the station wagon and van provided a very small load area and cost half as much again as the Beetle sedan, although it did preempt VW's first estate car by several years.

Hebmüller also produced a four-door open Beetle between 1947 and 1948, for police use: the Type 18A. The roof was removed, along with all the windows, and the factory windshield was replaced by a design that would eventually be used in the Cabriolet, which was sufficiently strong to secure the soft-top. The semaphore indicators were repositioned in the front quarter panels, and much reinforcing was added to the body and the chassis. Most of these cars simply had curtained openings for access instead of proper doors, although a handful were constructed using regular steel doors.

Standard police equipment included a gloss or matt pine green finish, a hand-operated spotlight, and a siren. Less than 400 of the Hebmüller police cars were built, and the last few were constructed after the Hebmüller fire, by Papler in Cologne, who had already been building their own four-door police Beetles. Obviously a popular choice among police forces, some 200 open four-door police Beetles, similar to the Papler design, were also produced by Austro-Tatra in Austria, between 1950 and 1951.

For the 1957 model year, the rear window was enlarged from its previous small oval shape to a rectangular shape. The front windshield was enlarged at the top and sides, and the window pillars became narrower. With this year, a new dashboard design was introduced, with the single instrument unit in front of the driver and a lidded glovebox on the passenger side, a layout which remained in a broadly similar form until the early 1990s. In December 1957, the two-millionth Volkswagen left the assembly line, and in 1959, the swing-axle pivot point was lowered by 0.6in. (15mm) by tipping the engine and transmission assembly two degrees forward, which in

LEFT: Ulf Kaijser's 1956 Beetle features nearly 50 genuine 1950s-style accessories. Not simply a show-car, the Oval has carried Ulf from his native Sweden, all across Europe.

BELOW LEFT: Dave Hammond's Polar Silver 1956 De Luxe Beetle was found in 1986 in a barn where it had been stored since 1979. Requiring only a mild restoration, the car had only 39,000 miles showing on the clock when it was discovered, and hasn't been out in the rain for the last eight years!

RIGHT: Part No. 111.012.025 – this rare toolkit was produced by German toolmakers Hazet, and was designed to fit into the spare wheel. The kit was available from the very early 1950s until 1966: this one dates from after 1958, as it includes a third small Phillips screwdriver for the fender-mounted indicator covers.

BELOW: Another view of the 1961 Beetle.

1954 VW 1200	
Engine	Air-cooled, four cylinder, horizontally-opposed, rear-mounted. Solex 28 PC1 carburetor.
Capacity	1192cc (72.7cu.in.)
Bore/stroke	77mm × 64mm (3.03in. × 2.52in.)
Output	30bhp @ 3400rpm
Compression ratio	6.1:1
Transmission	Four-speed transmission
Suspension type	Torsion bars, rear swing-axles
Brakes	Single-circuit, hydraulic, four drums
Top speed	67mph (108km/h)
Acceleration	0-50mph: 21.0secs
Fuel consumption	32.2mpg
Tires/wheels	4J × 15, 5.6 × 15 tires
Track front/rear	1290mm/1250mm
Wheelbase	2400mm (94.5in.)
Length	4070mm (160in.)
Width	1540mm (60.6in.)
Height	1500mm (59.1in.)
Unladen weight	730kg (1609lb)

conjunction with a front stabiliser improved the car's handling.

The 1960 model year saw the semaphore indicator arms disappear, replaced by indicator lamps mounted on the top of the front fenders and integrated within the rear taillight assembly. A raised compression ratio from 6.6:1 to 7.0:1 and a new Solex 28 PICT carburetor saw the power output of the 1192cc engine increased from 30bhp to a dizzy 34bhp, while pre-heating of the intake air improved cold running. The 1960 cars also benefited from a fully-synchronized transmission, and in 1961 the Beetle at last received a fuel gauge, doing away with the reserve tap, which could be turned when the car finally coughed to a halt, to give another few miles' worth of fuel; many owners had simply used a graduated stick to find out how much fuel they had left by dipping the tank.

The heating system was improved in 1962 to provide fume-free air, by using heat exchangers rather than simply passing the air over the engine cylinders as was previously the case. The following year, the optional large fabric soft-top was replaced by a smaller steel sliding version and the engine lid was reshaped slightly in order to use the licence plate light unit from the Type 3 cars. Larger front indicators were fitted, and the

1961 VW 1200

Engine	Air-cooled, four cylinder, horizontally-opposed, rear-mounted. Solex 28 PICT carburetor.
Capacity	1192cc (72.7cu.in.)
Bore/stroke	77mm × 64mm (3.03in. × 2.52in.)
Output	34bhp @ 3800rpm
Compression ratio	7.3:1
Transmission	Four-speed gearbox
Suspension type	Torsion bars, rear swing-axles
Brakes	Single-circuit, hydraulic, four drums
Top speed	71mph (115km/h)
Acceleration	0-62mph: 37.0secs
Fuel consumption	31.4mpg
Tires/wheels	4.5J × 15, 5.6 × 15 tires
Track front/rear	1308mm/1349mm (51.5in./53.1in.)
Wheelbase	2400mm (94.5in.)
Length	4060mm (160in.)
Width	1550mm (61.0in.)
Height	1500mm (59.1in.)
Unladen weight	760kg (1676lb)

RIGHT: This 1963 car shows the longer chrome strip on the hood which appeared after the Wolfsburg crest was discontinued in this year, and the narrow fender-mounted indicator lamps which replaced the semaphore arms in 1960.

BELOW RIGHT: A late 1950s Beetle engine. The vacuum advance for the distributor was introduced in 1953, and this engine features an aftermarket oil filter, seen on the top left of the engine compartment.

BELOW: This Belgian 1960 Cabriolet features the popular U.S.-spec. bumpers and the "fender skirts" over the rear wheel arches.

VW emblem in the hubcaps was no longer embossed in black.

In 1964, the rear window was again enlarged. This year it became some ⁸⁄₁₀in. (20mm) higher and ⁴⁄₁₀in. (10mm) wider, and the front windshield extended 1¹⁄₁₀in. (28mm) farther into the roof. The side windows were also enlarged, with slimmer pillars being used.

A new model was launched in 1965: the VW 1300, using a new 1285cc engine producing 40bhp. The front axle received ball-joints to replace the previous king and link-pin set-up, and perforated steel disk wheels, with new flatter hubcaps, were fitted.

The engine lid was changed again in 1966, to a shorter pressing with a new flat section to position the number plate more vertically in order to meet various international requirements; and in the same year another new model was launched:

the VW 1500, powered by a 44bhp 1493cc engine which pushed the Beetle to a top speed of 78mph (125km/h). The handling of all Beetle models was improved with the addition of an equalizing spring to the rear axle which reduced the "jacking-up" effect of the swing-axle suspension, and the new 1500 model was fitted as standard with front disk brakes.

New, stronger bumpers were introduced in 1967, their raised mounting height necessitating a shorter engine lid and hood, along with altered valances. The front fenders were also changed to use vertically-positioned headlights, and larger rear lights were introduced. The 1300/1500 models received a split-circuit braking system, and the 1500 model was also available with a semi-automatic transmission, where the driver shifted gear using a conventional gearlever, but with no clutch pedal – the clutch was actuated automatically when the lever was moved. The semi-automatic cars also used double-jointed rear axles: a more sophisticated rear suspension than the swing-axles found on the other models which reduced the camber effects during cornering – a trait which made fast driving difficult for the inexperienced. As the driver brakes in the swing-axle cars, the rear end tends to lift and the wheels tuck in – this raises the car's center of gravity and makes it more unstable.

The 34bhp 1200 model disappeared from the market in August 1967 for some six months, but returned under the name "Sparkäfer" or

RIGHT: These two classic VWs, a 1302S and a 1966 1300, are both owned by Gordon Sellars of Leicester, England. Gordon bought the '66 at 4800 miles, from the chief mechanic at his local Volkswagen dealership, and has since taken the mileage up to nearly 70,000 in 26 trouble-free years of ownership. Replacements have been limited to a new battery, a stainless steel silencer, new brake linings and a steering damper – Oh, and a new set of tires at 47,000 miles, although the original spare is still lurking under the front . . . unused!

1965 VW 1300

Engine	Air-cooled, four cylinder, horizontally-opposed, rear-mounted. Solex 28 PICT carburetor.
Capacity	1285cc (78.4cu.in.)
Bore/stroke	77mm × 69mm (3.03in. × 2.72in.)
Output	40bhp
Compression ratio	7.3:1
Transmission	Four-speed fully-synchronized transmission
Suspension type	Torsion bars, rear swing-axles
Brakes	Single-circuit, hydraulic, four drums
Top speed	75mph (120km/h)
Acceleration	0-62mph: 26.0secs
Fuel consumption	27.7mpg
Tires/wheels	4.5J × 15, 5.6 × 15 tires
Track front/rear	1316mm/1305mm (51.8in./51.4in.)
Wheelbase	2400mm (94.5in.)
Length	4030mm (159in.)
Width	1550mm (61.0in.)
Height	1500mm (59.1in.)
Unladen weight	820kg (1808lb)

"Economy Beetle," and remained available in this guise until the end of European production. This year also saw the big switch to 12-volt electrics, dramatically improving the power of the headlights over the feeble glimmer from the previous six-volt systems. A popular modification nowadays is the conversion from six to 12 volts, to provide better lighting and enable the use of modern audio equipment.

The late 1960s saw steady improvements in refinement, power and comfort without any radical changes in design. In 1968, the 1300 became available with the semi-automatic transmission and double-jointed rear suspension, and front disk brakes also became available as an option, these having previously been available only on the 1500 model.

The 1969-model-year Beetles can be identified by the increased number of louvers on the engine lid, necessitated by fitting the 1584cc, 47bhp engine from the Transporter into the U.S.-bound cars. In this year, the "L" package of options was introduced on the 1300 and 1500 models, comprising two reversing lights, rubber mouldings on the bumpers, a padded dashboard, anti-dazzle rear-view mirror, lockable glovebox, a mirror in the passenger sun visor, passenger door pocket, rear ashtray and loop pile carpets. All of these changes were relatively cosmetic, however, in comparison to the new model to come.

LEFT: 1965 saw the introduction of the 1300 model and ball-joint front suspension.

BELOW LEFT AND BELOW: The 1500 model was introduced in 1966; this 1967 example is fitted with the U.S.-spec. bumpers.

1966 VW 1500

Engine	Air-cooled, four cylinder, horizontally-opposed, rear-mounted. Solex 30 PICT carburetor.
Capacity	1493cc (91.1cu.in)
Bore/stroke	83mm × 69mm (3.27in. × 2.72in)
Output	44bhp
Compression ratio	7.5:1
Transmission	Four-speed fully-synchronized transmission
Suspension type	Torsion bars, rear swing-axles
Brakes	Single-circuit, hydraulic, four drums
Top speed	78mph (125km/h)
Acceleration	0-62mph: 23.0secs
Fuel consumption	26.7mpg
Tires/wheels	4.5J × 15, 5.6 × 15 tires
Track front/rear	1316mm/1305mm (51.8in./51.4in.)
Wheelbase	2400mm (94.5in.)
Length	4030mm (159in.)
Width	1550mm (61.0in.)
Height	1500mm (59.1in.)
Unladen weight	870kg (1918lb)

The Bug Gets Better

One of the major events in the production life of the Beetle came with the introduction of the new 1302 model in 1970. Marking the first real departure from Porsche's original designs, this model dispensed with the front torsion bar suspension in favor of MacPherson struts, and the rear suspension used double-jointed axles, as previously found only in conjunction with the semi-automatic transmission. The new front suspension resulted in a luggage area some 85% larger, and the 1302 was available with the 1200, 1300 or 1600 engines. This latter model was designated as the 1302S.

An increased compression ratio, twin inlet and exhaust ports, and improved oil cooling allowed the new redesigned 1300 engine to produce 44bhp, while similar changes to the 1600 unit resulted in an output of 50bhp. The engine lid was changed to accommodate the greater height of the two new engines, and all Beetles except the 1200 model received through-flow ventilation, with plastic crescent-shaped vents behind the rear side-windows.

The rear window got bigger yet again in 1971, this time by 1.6in. (4cm), and the engine lid now had 26 louvers. Inside, a new safety steering wheel with a deformable center and a removable cover over the rear luggage area, were fitted.

The Beetle reached a major milestone in 1972: on February 17, the 15,007,034th car left the production line, and the Beetle finally overtook the Model-T Ford to become the most-produced car in the world. To mark this special occasion, a limited-edition "World Champion" or "Weltmeister" Beetle was produced, also known as the "Marathon Beetle." Based on the 1300 model, these cars were finished in a special light blue metallic paint called Marathon Metallic. They featured special ten-spoke Lemmerz wheels, and a rubber strip in the bumpers. Owners were also given a commemorative medal reading "Der Weltmeister Wolfsburg Germany 1972." Around 1500 of these cars were imported into the U.K.,

PREVIOUS PAGES: Tony Blythe's Marino Yellow 1975 1200L is in fact powered by the optionally-available 1300 engine, and sits on the pressed-steel GT Beetle wheels. Clive Dixon's Tomato Red GT Beetle has only covered 60,000 miles since new.

LEFT: The 1972 Beetle.

RIGHT: The GT Beetle used the twin-port 50bhp, 1600cc engine.

BELOW: The 1302S was powered by the same engine, and used the MacPherson strut front suspension.

1970 VW 1302S

Engine	Air-cooled, four cylinder, horizontally-opposed, rear-mounted. Solex 30 PICT 3 carburetor.
Capacity	1584cc (96.7cu.in.)
Bore/stroke	85.5mm × 69mm (3.37in. × 2.72in.)
Output	50bhp @ 4000rpm
Compression ratio	7.5:1
Transmission	Four-speed fully-synchronized transmission
Suspension type	Front MacPherson struts, double jointed axles at rear
Brakes	Split circuit, hydraulic, four drums
Top speed	81mph (130km/h)
Acceleration	0-62mph: 22.5secs
Fuel consumption	27.7mpg
Tires/wheels	4.5J × 15, 5.6 × 15 tires
Track front/rear	1375mm/1352mm (54.1in./53.2in.)
Wheelbase	2420mm (95.3in.)
Length	4080mm (161in.)
Width	1585mm (62.4in.)
Height	1500mm (59.1in.)
Unladen weight	870kg (1918lb)

and all examples were snapped up at the price of £949.52.

In this year, a further and even more radical departure from Porsche's principles was unveiled, with the launch of the 1303 model. Using MacPherson strut front suspension and double-jointed rear axles as on the 1302 model, the 1303 also featured a sharply curved windshield, with the roof and scuttle moved farther forward and a shorter hood. Inside, the 1303 used a completely new and much larger dashboard, with full-width air vents. This was a response to suspected U.S. regulations concerning the distance of the driver's head from the windshield, which in the end, failed to materialize.

The 1972 model year also saw the import of the 300,000th car to the U.K. since 1953, and to commemorate this, 2500 of the 1300S model were imported and re-badged in the U.K. as a limited-edition GT Beetle. This was a traditional, torsion-bar, swing-axle, flat-windshield car – in other words, a "proper" Beetle – fitted with the 1600 engine, front disk brakes, special wheels made by Lemmerz and the larger rear lights from the 1303 cars. The GT Beetle also featured a special interior with beige cloth upholstery, a padded dashboard, wooden stick-shift top and a storage tray on the center tunnel. The cars were available only in three "fruity" colors: Lemon Yellow, Tomato Red and Apple Green. The GT Beetle retailed for £997, just £19 dearer than the standard 1300 model, and was the only U.K.

special-edition Beetle to have a special promotional brochure.

On July 1, 1974, the last Beetle produced in the Wolfsburg factory left the production line. Since 1945, 11,916,519 cars had been manufactured here, but production continued in the Hanover, Emden and Brussels factories. The Wolfsburg line then switched to production of the new Golf model, an all-new front-wheel drive, transverse-engined hatchback car which was to be such a success that it would spell the end of the line for the Beetle. In spite of this, the 18 millionth Beetle left the Emden line on October 4.

1974 was a good year for special-edition Beetles, with the line-up including the Big Beetle, the Jeans Beetle and the 1200 Super. The Big Beetle was based on the 1303S model, fitted with a wider version of the sports wheels used on the GT Beetle, and came in metallic paint with contrasting interior: Ontario Blue with blue interior, Moss Green with sand interior, Hellas Brown with brown trim, and Silver with blue trim. The cars also featured corduroy inserts on the seats, leather-effect steering wheel, wood grain dashboard panels, and a side stripe.

The Jeans Beetle was based on the 1200 model, finished in Tunis Yellow with a special "Jeans" decal on the side of the car and the engine lid. The car used the same sports wheels as the GT Beetle and the interior was trimmed in a blue denim-look fabric with orange stitching. Yet another special edition for 1974 was the 1200 Super, which was available only in Marino Yellow and Phoenix Red, and was a 1200 Beetle with full headlining, rubber bumper strips, chrome door handle finger plates, black leatherette seat covers with cloth inserts and the GT Beetle wheels.

Partly as a result of the highly successful introduction of the Golf, the Beetle range was cut down again in 1975: the 1302 and 1303 models were discontinued, leaving only the flat-screen, torsion-bar, swing-axle models; although the 1303 body style would be available in Cabriolet form until 1979. Although the 1302 and 1303 cars

ABOVE LEFT: The "Jeans" Beetle was a special edition for 1974.

ABOVE: The new larger rear lights were introduced in 1972.

RIGHT: The 1303 was launched in 1972, using MacPherson strut front suspension and a curved windshield.

OVERLEAF: With the launch of the 1303, the Karmann Cabriolet adopted the same body until the end of Cabriolet production.

1973 VW 1303

Engine	Air-cooled, four cylinder, horizontally-opposed, rear-mounted, Solex 34 PICT 3 carburetor.
Capacity	1285cc (78.4cu.in.)
Bore/stroke	77mm × 69mm (3.03in. × 2.72in.)
Output	44bhp
Compression ratio	7.5:1
Transmission	Four-speed fully-synchronized transmission
Suspension type	Front MacPherson struts, double jointed axles at rear
Brakes	Split circuit, hydraulic, four drums
Top speed	78mph (125km/h)
Acceleration	0-62mph: 25.5secs
Fuel consumption	26.7mpg
Tires/wheels	4.5J × 15, 5.6 × 15 tires
Track front/rear	1316mm/1305mm (51.8in./51.4in.)
Wheelbase	2420mm (95.3in.)
Length	4110mm (162in.)
Width	1585mm (62.4in.)
Height	1500mm (59.1in.)
Unladen weight	890kg (1962lb)

enjoy a considerable following and are in many ways more practical, they are shunned by some enthusiasts as not being a "proper" Beetle as originally envisaged by Dr. Porsche. The Beetle was now available only with 1200 or 1600 engines, although the "L" option pack remained available.

The departure of the 1303 was marked with a special-edition "Campaign" model produced at the end of the 1975 model year. These cars were finished in metallic brown (hence their nickname "Chocolate Beetle") and were fitted as standard with extra chrome trim and the GT Beetle wheels. Alongside the Campaign model was the Sun Beetle, based on the 1300 model with a steel sliding sunroof, the sports wheels, padded dashboard and heated rear window. The Sun Beetles were available only in Sun Yellow or Sun Orange.

In September, Volkswagen announced another car which was to take the motoring world by storm – although not to the same extent as the Beetle. The Golf GTi, which was to inspire similar cult status and enthusiasm, would spawn imitators from just about every other major manufacturer, and gave birth to a completely new category of car – the hot-hatchback.

The Beetle remained in production in this form until 1978, a year engraved with sorrow in the minds of many European enthusiasts: in January, European production of the Beetle ceased, and cars were imported to Germany from the Mexican factory. However, the left-hand drive Mexican-produced cars were not imported to the U.K., and so 1978 marked the end of the Beetle for Britain, with nearly 500,000 Volkswagens having been sold since Colborne Garages began importing Beetles in 1952.

John Colborne-Baber had been specializing in Beetles since 1950, when he had become the official concessionaire for Volkswagen spares in Britain, and was granted the license to import complete cars in 1952, which were sold to U.S. servicemen stationed in the country, earning much-needed U.S. dollars. The car which originally drew John Colborne-Baber's attention to the Beetle was manufactured in 1947, and was brought to England by a Swedish visitor: the car is still owned by Colborne Garages, and John's son Peter regularly uses the Beetle, registered JLT 420, today.

The end of official Beetle imports to the U.K. was commemorated with a special "Last Edition" model. A special batch of 600 cars was produced, based on the 1200L. About half of these were finished in the standard colors – Alpine White, Riyad Yellow, Miami Blue and Mars Red, but the very last 300 cars were finished in Diamond Silver metallic and were fitted with a special numbered plaque on the dashboard.

Mexican versions differed from the German-produced cars in several respects. The cars used the smaller rear windows as used on German-produced cars between 1965 and 1971, and the alternator of the later European cars was replaced by a generator. Available only with the 1200 engine, Mexican cars featured side trim, fuel gauge, heated rear window, anti-dazzle mirror, passenger grab handle, inertia-reel seatbelts and adjustable headrests. The running board trims and the tailpipes were once again chrome plated.

A further blow was dealt to Beetle enthusiasts on January 10, 1979, when the Cabriolet was discontinued to make way for the Golf Cabriolet at the Karmann plant in Osnabrück. Over 31 years, the Karmann plant had produced 330,281 cars, making the Beetle Cabriolet the most-produced open car in the world.

On May 15, 1981, the 20 millionth Beetle was produced, and to mark the occasion, a special edition "Silver Bug" was produced, with silver metallic paintwork and special "20 Millionen" badging on the engine lid, the gear shift and the matching key ring. But this was not the only special edition to appear in the early 1980s. Between 1982 and 1984, the Mexican plant produced several special models, mostly variations in paint and trim colours. These included the Jeans Bug and Special Bug in 1982, the Aubergine Beetle and Ice Blue Beetle in 1983, and the Sunny Bug and Velvet Red Beetle in 1984.

In 1985, the Beetle celebrated its 50th birthday, and the "Jubilee Beetle" or Jubilaumskäfer was produced to mark the event. This was finished in Pewter Grey metallic paint with tinted green windows, and used the larger rear

RIGHT: This 1303 Cabriolet rides on replica Porsche alloy wheels.

BELOW: A 1984 Mexican Beetle, finished in Mars Red.

window as seen on post-'72 European cars together with the bulged rear apron as on post-'75 European cars, while the interior included GTi-style seats, upholstery and steering wheel. Externally, the Jubilaumskäfer was distinguished by sports wheels and special "50 Jahre" badging, and this model also marked the end of exports to Germany – the Beetle was finally officially unavailable in Europe. Since 1978, U.K. enthusiasts had been importing cars from Germany, but buying a new Beetle now involved rather more than a simple trip across the Channel. However, a trickle of personally-imported cars continued to make their way across the Atlantic, and a surprisingly large number of Brazilian and Mexican cars are running around on European roads.

Now that they no longer had to cater for the requirements of export markets, the Mexican factory were able to make several modifications to the Beetle design after 1985, mostly to minimize production costs and optimize the car for local conditions, although some of the Mexican modifications are definitely "upgrades." In 1985, the rear heating outlets were discontinued, the hood lid and engine lid seals were mounted on the lids rather than on the body, halogen headlamps were introduced and the rear sound

LEFT: The later Mexican models used an electric washer pump.

BELOW LEFT: The interior of this Jubilee Beetle features non-standard wooden dashboard inserts.

ABOVE: The special "50 Jahre" badge on the rear of the Jubilee Beetle.

BELOW: A Cal-look Beetle in the classic style, this 1962 example reputedly cost the owner nearly $20,000 to complete, and was built specifically to win shows.

deadening material was deleted, along with the heated rear window.

For 1986, an intermittent wash/wipe was available, and in 1988, the fresh air ventilation system was deleted and small plastic center caps replaced the metal hubcaps. Electronic ignition was fitted in 1988 and an alarm became standard in 1990. For the 1991 model year, the AF-series engine was fitted with a two-way exhaust catalyst with the rear apron being modified to suit the new single tail-pipe. At the same time, the chrome trim for front and rear windows was discontinued and a new style of dashboard was introduced, with a lower radio mounting position and Golf-style switches. A special taxi model was also introduced.

Production at the Brazilian Volkswagen factory, which was established in Sao Paulo in 1953 and produced Beetles since January 1959, ceased in 1986, and despite repeated rumors that production was also to cease at the Mexican factory (which had been producing cars since 1967) the car gained a new lease of life in 1991 when the Mexican government announced a road tax exemption for cars sold below a certain price. The Beetle was the only car to sell below this threshold, and sales increased from 33,000 in 1989 to 86,000 in 1991.

Production has continued at about 450 cars a day ever since, and on June 23, 1992, with a sur-

prising lack of publicity, Beetle No. 21,000,000 left the Puebla production line, again celebrated by a special edition of some 6000 – in this case with "21 Milliones" badging. The 1992 model Beetles were fitted with a new padded steering wheel, dual-circuit brakes with a warning light, inertia reel front seatbelts, static rear seatbelts and a new windshield washer bottle fitted to the left of the fuel tank – previous Mexican cars having used a bottle with integral electric pump, mounted in the spare wheel. A new GL model was introduced for this year, using a sports steering wheel, older (pre-'91) style wheels with chrome hubcaps, passenger door mirror, rear parcel shelf, new front boot lining and radio speakers in the doors.

Changes for the 1993 model year included the adoption of Digifant fuel injection and regulated catalytic converter. They also introduced hydraulic tappets, dual valve springs, and at long last, a proper oil filter. In 1993, rumors abounded that the Brazilian factory may begin producing the Beetle again, for similar reasons to the Mexicans. Indeed it has even been whispered that the car may be reintroduced to Europe in small numbers as an alternative to the astronomical development costs of a modern small car, and as a result of the growing desire for more individualistic transport in a world of automotive conformity. The appeal of the Beetle is as strong as ever.

Beetle Derivatives

TYPE 2

Although the Volkswagen empire had been built on the success of the Beetle, the range was being expanded as early as 1948, when the first "Type 2" vans were produced (the Beetle is Volkswagen Type 1), following a suggestion by Ben Pon on a visit to the factory in his capacity as the Dutch VW importer. He noticed some rather rough-and-ready platform trucks which were used to ferry loads around the factory, and which comprised a Beetle floorpan chassis with an upright cab at the rear over the engine, and a load-carrying platform at the front. Seeing the efficiency of these factory transport vehicles, he scribbled a rough sketch in his notebook, of a Volkswagen-based commercial vehicle which followed similar principles, but with the driver's cab mounted at the front.

The first prototypes were built using a modified Beetle floorpan, but this proved unsatisfactory, and so a new approach was developed, using a totally new chassis with a central spine and outriggers to the sills. This gave a sturdy platform to which the body was welded, creating an integral body and chassis, unlike the Beetle with its removable body. The mechanical parts were basically as used on the Beetle: the same engine and transmission were used, mounted in a similar mounting fork arrangement at the rear of the chassis, and the torsion bar suspension was used at the front.

The first prototype van used a standard Beetle transmission, but when the standard 25bhp Beetle engine of the time, unsurprisingly, struggled with the task of pushing along a fully-laden commercial vehicle, the engineers raided their parts bins and discovered that a reduction box system, similar to that which had been employed on the wartime Kübelwagen, provided the van with usefully reduced gearing. This enabled it to climb 1 in 4 gradients even at its maximum payload of 15cwt.

The new van was launched in 1950, to a warm reception from customers; it was a radically different proposition from the rather agricultural vans of this size offered by rival manufacturers, and in effect established a niche market. The panel van was soon joined by the "Kombi" – a panel van with three windows in each side, optional rear seats and spartan interior; and then by the "Microbus," offering a more comfortable specification. The range was widened further in 1951 with the introduction of the "Deluxe Microbus," which featured exterior chrome trims and a rear bumper among other things, with four windows per side and a window on each rear corner. The Deluxe could also be ordered with a full-length fabric sliding roof, and a total of eight tinted skylight windows; these "23-window" Microbuses are very much sought-after today.

Alongside the panel van and the buses, many variations on the basic Type 2 were produced, including a pick-up version, a double-cab pick-up

and numerous specially-built vehicles. Updates to the original design meant that by the time a new model was introduced in 1967, the Type 2 boasted a 1500cc, 42bhp engine and 12-volt electrics.

The new model launched in 1967 featured a wraparound front windshield and completely new body styling, although a resemblance to the original design remained. With various alterations, this model, beloved of Antipodean travelers, was produced until the introduction of a new, squarer-shaped model in 1979. The rear-engined layout, with options ranging from turbo-diesels to a 2100cc fuel-injected unit, remained until 1991, when a new generation of front-engined Transporters were introduced.

PREVIOUS PAGES AND TOP LEFT: A 1962 motor caravan, complete with elevating roof. The Type 2s also featured a large VW emblem on the front.

LEFT AND BELOW LEFT: This particular caravan conversion dates from 1962, and features an immalculate interior.

ABOVE: For those needing space for passengers and a load bed, the Crew-cab pick-up was the answer; this is a 1961 example of this rare model.

RIGHT: The Type 2 was facelifted in 1968 to give a more rounded body style with a single wraparound windshield. This 1978 example was imported into the U.K. from France.

LEFT AND BELOW LEFT: The Karmann Ghia Cabriolet and Coupe. The Coupe is a 1958 model, and the Cabriolet dates from 1968.

ABOVE RIGHT: The Karmann Ghia was designed by Ghia, and produced for VW by Karmann.

BELOW: Even the Karmann Ghia sees it fair share of customizing – but whether the flames really suit these classic handbuilt lines is very much a question of personal preference!

KARMANN GHIA

As early as 1950, executives from Karmann, the German coachbuilding firm who were already producing the four-seater VW convertible, had been discussing with VW the possibility of producing a sporting convertible based on the Beetle chassis. Several designs and styling models were submitted to Wolfsburg by the Karmann artists, but were rejected as not quite capturing the essence of what the VW chiefs had in mind for their sportscar. A meeting between Wilhelm Karmann and Luigi Segre, President of the Italian styling house Carrozzeria Ghia, saw Segre agree to produce a prototype for the proposed VW-based sportscar. Purchasing a Beetle from a friend who was the French importer for VW, Segre took the car to the Ghia works in Turin, where it was bodied according to the designs he had made in the meantime. The finished design was then presented to the Vice-President of Volkswagen, Dr. Feuereisen, in 1953 and met with enthusiastic approval – the Volkswagen Karmann Ghia was born.

Although the Karmann Ghia was based on the Export Beetle chassis, certain modifications were necessary; the central tunnel was retained, together with the front suspension and steering, and the engine and transmission, but a new floor structure was added, some 4.6in. (118mm) wider than the Beetle, together with new sills and other reinforcements.

For production of the car, Export-model Beetle chassis were supplied by Volkswagen to Karmann, who produced the bodies, complete with the interiors, and assembled the cars, which were then distributed through the Volkswagen network. Production began in August 1955, and the first 37 cars were delivered to dealers in August 1956, but orders soon speeded up, and in the next 14 months, some 10,000 were produced.

Work on a convertible version of the coupé began almost immediately. The removal of the roof required no changes to the exterior sheet-metal below the waistline of the car, and Ghia was not called in this time, although considerable reinforcing of the lower bodywork was necessary. Production of the Karmann Ghia convertible began in August 1957.

The Karmann Ghia was always the most luxurious model in the air-cooled range, and like the Beetle convertible, it used the most luxurious interior specifications and the latest mechanical refinements as soon as they were introduced to the Beetle range. However, it was never a real sportscar – contemporary U.S. advertising even showed the car unable to break through a paper sheet, and it was sold more as a stylish Beetle than a sporting model. Another advertisement proclaimed the Karmann Ghia a car "For people who can't stand the sight of a Volkswagen." In total, some 364,398 Type 1 Karmann Ghias – 80,897 convertible and 283,501 coupés – were produced, along with a further 23,577 cars in the Brazilian Karmann factory. These were also based on the Beetle, but the Brazilian cars used a rather different "fastback" body.

Production of the Type 1 Karmann Ghia was ended in July 1974, when the Beetle was due to be phased out in favor of the new water-cooled cars, and so it was thought that the chassis would not be available for long (little did they know that some 20 years later, Beetles would still be leaving the Puebla factory!). In addition, VW's new sportscar, the Golf-based Scirocco, also built by Karmann, and effectively superseding the Karmann Ghia, was ready for launch.

THESE PAGES: The Karmann Ghia Cabriolet was introduced in 1957. This particular example features a re-trimmed interior and has U.S.-style bumpers.

LEFT: The relatively rare "notchback" version of the Type 3 was never a big seller.

RIGHT: For the Type 3, the fan was mounted on the end of the crankshaft to give a lower profile, allowing the engine to slip under the rear load floor.

BELOW: The Type 3 – intended originally to replace the Beetle, the car used a "flat" version of the air-cooled engine, and provided luggage space in both ends.

TYPE 3

With Volkswagen relying on the Beetle as its main product, criticism began to be levelled at Nordhoff; many industry observers found it incredible that the firm was still relying on a pre-war design, as late as 1957. When asked in that year when a replacement for the Beetle would be introduced, he is quoted as saying "Can anybody seriously believe that we will change this car, which has scored so many successes? You can rest assured that I shall not make this mistake. We shall concentrate on eradicating gradually and positively all those small and large design errors, inevitable in any car, and this is what we are doing." By profession, Nordhoff was an engineer, not a marketing professional, and was accused by critics, of having created in Volkswagen "the sleeping giant of Wolfsburg." In fact, Nordhoff was not sticking doggedly and imprudently to a "one-model" policy as was claimed by critics; Porsche engineers had in fact been working on a Beetle replacement as early as 1953, and by 1957, the design specification had been pretty well finalized.

Despite having been initiated so long ago, this Beetle replacement was constantly delayed simply because every time Nordhoff attempted to set a date for the introduction of the new car, he looked to the Beetle sales statistics – which in the 1950s were sufficiently buoyant to discourage him from superseding the car. However, Nordhoff realized that the time for a new model must come eventually, and so cautiously, he introduced the new car, known as the Type 3, alongside the Beetle.

The new car had to provide more interior space than the Beetle, but with the same wheelbase, which resulted in a squarer body shape than the Beetle. Nordhoff's insistence that the new car would be available also as a station wagon (Variant) meant that a new low-profile engine needed to be developed, which could be fitted in the rear of the car yet still allow a load-space above it; this would have been impossible with the standard Beetle engine, using the vertical fan mounted above the crankcase.

The solution was typically neat, and involved using a 1500cc version of the Volkswagen air-cooled engine, with a smaller diameter fan, mounted on the rear end of the crankshaft, with the generator driven by a belt from the pulley at the flywheel end of the crankshaft. Similar suspension arrangements to the Beetle were employed, with torsion bars used at the front and swing-axles at the rear, and the backbone chassis was based on that of the Beetle. Using the low-profile engine gave the car two trunks; one above the engine at the rear, and one under the hood at the front.

The Type 3 sedan and Variant entered production in September 1961, and the cars were initially offered with a 45bhp version of the new 1493cc engine. Although in August 1963, a deluxe version, the 1500S, was introduced,

featuring a higher compression ratio (8.5:1) and twin Solex 32 PDSIT carburetors, which saw the power output boosted to 54bhp. The standard model stayed with a single carburetor and became the 1500N.

The 1965 model year saw the introduction of a third body style to the Type 3 range, with the introduction of the VW 1600TL - a "fastback" version of the sedan model, using a new 1584cc version of the "pancake" engine, which then became standard across the Type 3 range. The new power unit also used dual Solex 32 PDSIT carburetors, and although it developed no more outright power, it did provide better power at lower engine speeds.

In conjunction with the larger engine, the 1966 model year saw the Type 3 cars fitted with front disk brakes. This year also saw the introduction of the Type 3 in Variant and Fastback form, to the U.S. The car had only been available previously in Canada, although many of the new Type 3 cars had already found their way to the U.S. through this route.

However, over half of the Type 3 cars sold were Variants, underlining the fact that the car was bought mostly for its practicality, and that the aim of luring buyers upmarket from the Beetle had not really succeeded. The model received a slight facelift in 1969, but production ended in 1973.

TYPE 3 KARMANN GHIA

With the development of the Type 3 cars, Nordhoff approached Karmann to produce a coupé and convertible version of the new car, to run alongside the original Karmann Ghia models. The main designer of the car was Sergio Sartorelli, and the chief body engineer was Johannes Beeskow, already famous for his 1951 Römetsch design. Several suggestions have been made over the years, however, that the shape of the car was heavily influenced by the Chevrolet Corvair. The Type 3 Karmann Ghia coupé, VW Type 34, went into production in 1962, although the convertible never made it past the prototype stage. The technical specifications of the cars mirrored that of the Type 3 sedan models, with the cars receiving twin-carburetor versions of the 1500cc engine and then a 1600cc unit. Production of the Type 3 Karmann Ghia ended in June 1969, with a total of 42,434 having been built.

TYPE 4: 411/412

The year of Nordhoff's death, 1968, saw a radical change in the Volkswagen model strategy. Top management at Wolfsburg had decided to go upmarket and produce a luxury car which would still cling to the rear-engined air-cooled ethos, but which would offer space and refinement unheard of with the Beetle. The result was the Type 4, or 411 as the model was designated, following its prototype codename. Although the engine was air-cooled and was behind the passengers, this was about the only similarity with previous Volkswagens, for the 411 ushered in a significant number of technical innovations for VW.

Realizing that the Beetle chassis was limited in terms of its future development potential, the Wolfsburg engineers created their first unitary-construction, monocoque bodyshell, using a wheelbase of 98.4in (2500mm) against the Beetle and Type 3 at 94.5in. (2400mm). The 411 was the first European VW to offer four doors, and the suspension used MacPherson struts at the front, similar to the forthcoming 1302/1303 Beetles, with double-jointed trailing arms at the rear.

Although the styling strayed into the bland side of design, the 411 seems at first sight to be a pretty cunning package. The car offered more luggage space than the Type 3, more comfortable interiors available as standard or deluxe right from the start, and a standard auxiliary petrol-fired heater; but it was never the success it was meant to be. Initially offered with a 1700cc engine and dual carburetors, but offering only 68bhp, the 411 was a heavy car and the performance was fairly modest as a result. The 411 was also the most expensive Volkswagen, and was outclassed at its price level.

The criticism of the mediocre performance was addressed in 1969 with the introduction of the fuel-injected 411E (Einspritz) model, offering 80bhp, and a host of other modifications to the engine including new cylinder heads and pistons. The engine subsequently grew to 1800cc and the model received a new nose, but by the time the 1974 model was announced in 1973, the car was into its second facelift in just four years, and had even gained a new model designation – the 412E. Clearly lagging behind the competition, and even outclassed by VW's own K70 and the Audi 100 – also from VW's own stable – the Type 4 eventually ended production in 1974 after just 400,000 had been produced in its six-year lifespan – a drop in the ocean by VW production standards.

LEFT AND BELOW RIGHT: The 412 was a facelifted version of the 411; this example is an estate version, offically named "Variant."

BELOW LEFT: This 1965 Type 3 Karmann Ghia features a non-standard color scheme; the show-winning car was originally white with a black roof.

VW-PORSCHE 914

Perhaps the ultimate development of the Beetle idea, the Porsche 914 used the 1700cc, 80bhp engine from the Type 4, mounted in a mid-engined configuration in a low-slung two-seater sportscar. The car was largely a Porsche design, and was sold as the 914/4 with the VW engine, and as the 914/6 with a 110bhp Porsche six-cylinder unit. The cars were sold through a joint VW-Porsche marketing concern, which gave rise to speculation about Porsche being swallowed up by the VW empire. The car later received the 1800cc version of the VW engine, and eventually it was given a two-liter power-unit. At this point the sales began to take off, with the 914/4 offering almost as much performance (with a top speed of nearly 112mph) as the 914/6 but for less money. The 914 was produced until 1975, with 115,646 having been fitted with a VW engine.

181

The 411 was not the only new VW in 1969, but the company's second new arrival could hardly have been more different. In the 1960s, the Bundeswehr, the West German army, wanted a robust cross-country vehicle to use alongside their existing fleets of DKW Mungas. Volkswagen was enlisted to provide the development work, and the result was the Beetle-based Type 181. Since the army wanted initially only about 15,000 vehicles, Volkswagen attempted to offset some of the production costs by making the vehicle available as a civilian model. Marketed as "The Thing" in the U.S., the "Trekker" in the U.K., and the "Safari" in Mexico, this was a multi-purpose off-road utility vehicle in the mold of the warime Kübelwagen.

Using a boxy body on a modified Karmann Ghia floorpan, and powered by a detuned version of the 1500cc Beetle engine, the 181 lacked four-wheel drive (although a locking differential was optionally available), but gained increased ground clearance and lower gearing through using reduction boxes on the rear axles, similar to the early Type 2 models and the Kübelwagen. The front axle was a reinforced version of that used in the Beetle. The 181 was fitted with a folding hood made from PVC, and along with four removable steel doors, the windows were removable, and the windshield could be folded forward.

Very few modifications were made to the 181 during its lifespan, but in 1970, a low-compression 1600cc engine was fitted giving 44bhp (this was later increased to 48bhp). Fresh-air heating using heat exchangers was available in 1974, with large intake pods added to the rear fenders as a result. In addition, the reduction boxes were dispensed with in favor of the double-jointed rear suspension of the 1302. The U.S.-market cars produced in the Mexican plant were fitted with the large "elephant's foot" rear lights from the 1303 after 1973.

Built to a military contract, the 181 was of course not developed with any reference to cost-saving and consequently cost almost as much as the Type 4. The car was extremely spartan inside, yet gained popularity with construction workers and the like, and was produced until 1978. Production included some 26,531 complete cars, and 44,175 CKD kits which were assembled in the Mexican plant, mostly for export to the U.S. On the close of German production in 1978, the Mexican factory produced complete cars until 1980. In addition, some 6,500 cars were assembled from CKD kits in Indonesia.

COUNTRY BUGGY

A similar no-frills concept to the beach buggies, the Country Buggy, was produced in South Australia. The Australian VW plant was opened in Clayton in 1954, and assembled Beetles from CKD kits. By the 1960s, the possibility of manufacturing a utility vehicle geared to Australian conditions, was being discussed. Officially named the "Country Buggy," the resulting vehicle was based on the Beetle, with an appallingly ugly body fabricated from sheet steel to keep tooling costs down. A simple soft-top and side screens offered rudimentary weather protection, and three models were offered: a 1200cc, 34bhp version in right-hand drive, and two 1300cc, 40bhp versions in both right- and left-hand drive form. Only 1956 Country Buggies were manufactured between 1968 and 1972, its lack of success perhaps a result of its home-built appearance.

ABOVE RIGHT: This 181 has retained its NATO-style military paintwork in civilian life.

ABOVE AND RIGHT: The VW-Porsche 914 used the four-cylinder engine from the VW Type 4 cars or a 6-cylinder Porsche unit. These examples are of the Porsche-engined 914/6 type.

From Street to Strip

Since the earliest efforts of specialist coach-builders such as Hebmüller and Karmann, enthusiast home builders realized the enormous potential of the VW chassis as a fully-functional rolling chassis to which any kind of purpose-built body could be attached. Although the standard bodywork adds rigidity, the chassis is pretty well self-contained, and can even be driven around under its own steam.

One of the best-known types of kit car is the beach buggy; originating, as you might expect, in Southern California, where Beetles were stripped to the bare bones for desert or sand dune use. At first, people rode around the dunes on what was pretty much a bare chassis, with a few roll bars added in strategic places, but it wasn't long until a few simple body shapes were produced to attach to the chassis. The man generally credited with the idea of the beach buggy is Californian Bruce Meyers, and his Meyers Manx buggy first hit the beach in 1964.

The idea subsequently returned to West Germany, where the specialist VW magazine *Gute Fahrt* published a design in 1969 which was subsequently produced and marketed by Karmann as the "GF" in a kit for home assembly. The kit included the GRP body, and all the other parts to build a finished buggy, except for the chassis, axles and engine. The "GF" used a shortened Beetle chassis, and around 1500 kits were sold – some were even assembled by Karmann as fully-built cars using brand new parts.

Since then, countless buggy designs have been produced. with the first British-built buggy appearing in 1967 as the Volksrod, hotly followed by the GP Buggy. Indeed, such is the enduring appeal of the beach buggy concept that both these designs are still in production. Of course, the kit car concept is not limited to beach buggies. Kit cars designed to use the VW chassis have ranged from sportscars to delivery vans, and many "replica" bodies are available to give the VW that vintage feel.

One of the most popular designs was the Nova which originated in the 1970s and featured an entire lifting roof canopy instead of conventional doors; and several kits styled loosely after Lamborghini, Ferrari and even Bugatti models are available. In the early 1980s, UVA introduced the Montage, styled after the McLaren M42, and some of the more popular kits on the scene include the Avante, Eagle, Bonito, Karma, Talon, Tornado and Charger. To take things one stage further, the Covin kit provides an almost exact copy of the Porsche 911 bodyshell.

Of course, while it may look to the casual observer like a Ferrari or Bugatti, it will always be pretty obvious when the car is fired up that it's a VW flat-four in the tail, and not Ettore's finest, sitting behind the radiator of a genuine Type 52. However, one "replica" body kit which is pretty close to the real thing is the Porsche 356 kit available from several manufacturers.

The early Porsche sportscars were built for the most part using Beetle parts, and the 356 is very close to the Beetle in terms of its mechanical specification. Although the bodyshells may be fiberglass, most of them are of a very high quality and it takes more than a casual glance to determine whether the car is a genuine Porsche 356 Speedster or a fiberglass shell on a Beetle body. A similar concept is the replica of the Porsche RS 550 Spyder (the model known to many as that in which James Dean met his end), and with a little tuning, these Beetle-based cars can often be considerably faster than the original Porsche model.

The no-frills concept of the beach buggy was taken a step further with the advent of the "sand rail" – really just a tube-framed chassis with an engine, seats and four wheels. These were first developed for sand racing, but these days a road-legal version can be bought from several sources.

Off-road racing in the U.S. also gave rise to the "Baja" Beetle, named after the famous "Baja 1000" race in Mexico. Desert racers would remove large sections of the car's front and rear bodywork in order to increase ground clearance when climbing hills, and eventually fiberglass sections were

PREVIOUS PAGES: This Baja Bug is intended for serious off-road use, as shown by the knobbly tires and the roof-mounted oil cooler.

BELOW: This high-riding Baja Bug, complete with 1970s-style paintwork, is intended for the street, rather than off-road use.

BOTTOM: This Beetle has been altered with a fiberglass kit, intended to ape the Porsche 911.

RIGHT: The "sand rail" began in California, and amounts to little more than a tubular frame with a seat and a Beetle engine.

BELOW RIGHT: The Wizard is a U.K.-built roadster conversion for the Beetle. Not happy with just a roadster, the owner of this car has added Ferrari Testarossa-style side strakes.

produced to finish off the rough edges. The "Baja" style has grown in popularity and many street-driven Beetles have been customized to give this off-road look.

Such is the innovative spirit in the VW industry that the kit car business has now come full-circle, with the production of complete fiberglass bodies. The idea is the brainchild of Peter Cheeseman, whose business, Wizard Roadsters, had for several years been producing two- and four-seat cabriolet conversion kits for the Beetle sedan. As the supply of solid, rust-free cars began to dry up, Peter began producing complete fiberglass bodies, and these are available as either a standard sedan or convertible; taking this route means never having to worry about rust again!

The urge to be different, a desire for ostentation which is, of course, totally at odds with the whole ethos of the Beetle, has been present ever since the first simple accessory was produced back in postwar Germany; and the Beetle custom scene has now evolved into a major industry, with most of the impetus coming from the U.S.

Fads come and go, but one customizing style which has stuck around for longer than the rest

is the California Look, referred to as the "Cal-look." Formally recognized in 1975 by the Californian magazine, *Hot VWs*, the Cal-look began as one of the most simple and subtle forms of Beetle customizing, but has now become so popular that the term Cal-look has come to be used to describe more or less any lowered Beetle.

The Cal-look originally involved a few key features: a lowering job, removal of the chrome trim, aftermarket wheels – usually one of just a few select designs – and often, a hot engine. Most of the customized Beetles to be seen nowadays are variations on the basic theme of the Cal-look, although many cash-starved owners never seem to get beyond the stage of removing the bumpers, hence the number of bumperless Beetles to be seen on the roads these days.

Since the first Volkswagens were tried out in drag-race meetings in the 1960s, where modestly-tuned Beetles humiliated Detroit V8's, the Beetle has come to be a familiar sight at drag-strips worldwide; and although VW drag racing is often a serious business, this relatively cheap sport provides a chance for everyone to have a go, in the true spirit of the People's Car.

The origins of the Beetle's amazing success and popularity in the field of drag-racing can be found in 1960s America, where a few enthusiasts saw how the class structures of the sport could be exploited by a Beetle with the right engine. At first, the Beetle was regarded as a joke on the drag racing scene; a 30bhp family car was hardly a machine to terrify V8 racers! However, tuning parts could already be obtained, thanks to imports of the German Okrasa kits, and together with a few U.S.-manufactured parts, a fairly powerful engine could be built.

Thanks to the class structures of the sport, the Beetles suddenly started winning races – helped by the traction benefits of their rear-engined configuration. One of the earliest and most successful of these drag cars was the "Inch Pincher," which was built by Joe Vittone, the founder of the Californian EMPI firm, which was to become a major player in the Beetle speed and custom scene for many years to come.

The early drag-racing Beetles were only mildly modified, but constant development over the years led to drag-racing Beetles reaching speeds of over 110mph; and although the drag Beetles of the 1960s tended to be virtually standard apart from the engine, wheels and tires, the search for greater power and lighter weight soon changed this. Nowadays, the factory floorpan is often replaced with purpose-built lightweight tube chassis, and the steel Beetle body is replaced in whole or part with fiberglass replica panels.

At the ultimate end of the scale are the "Funny cars," where the engine is usually mounted in front of the driver, in a tube chassis, covered with

BELOW: Not what you'd expect to find lurking under the engine lid of the average pre-'56 VW; this twin-carbureted unit has been fully "dressed-up" with lashings of chrome.

BOTTOM: Emanating from California (where else!), this 1969 Beetle is some 18 inches thinner than standard.

RIGHT: This striking yellow Cal-look car features graphics and EMPI-style wheels.

BELOW RIGHT: This vivid purple Cal-look Beetle is the owner of the engine shown below.

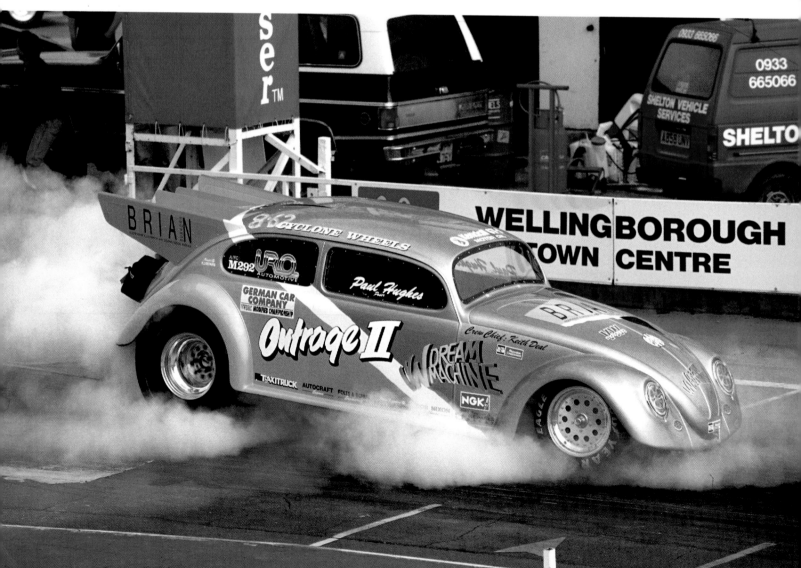

LEFT: This Oval-window car has been extensively modified to take to the strip.

BELOW LEFT: The "burnout" is used to warm up the tires for maximum traction.

ABOVE: Craig Winstanley's "Fugitive" drag-racing sandrail.

ABOVE RIGHT: A Californian drag-racer attacks the quarter-mile.

a fiberglass body which only vaguely resembles a Beetle. Such cars often use nitrous oxide injection and turbocharging, and reach up to 180mph, turning in quarter-mile times as low as nine seconds.

The craze for speed doesn't stop on the dragstrip, either: there's even a land speed record for a Beetle, achieved at Bonneville Salt Flats using a street-legal car which was able to post a record speed of 132mph – a real achievement when you consider that this car had to run for several miles at high speed, unlike the often frail drag-racing engines, which can be run only for a few seconds.

The VW drag racing scene kicked off in the U.K. back in 1987, when Brett Hawksbee organized the first "Bug Jam" at the Santa Pod dragstrip, in order to provide a U.S.-style one-day event for those younger VW enthusiasts hungry for the type of events they had been reading about in the Californian magazines. The event included a "Run What Ya Brung" class, to allow everyone to try their own car down the strip: a standard 1200 Beetle hardly provides a kick in the back down the strip, but who knows that, when you can go home and tell your friends you've been "racing" for the day?

The success of "Bug Jam" led to the formation of the VW Drag Racing Club (VWDRC), and the scene has gone from strength to strength ever since, with many purpose-built VW-based dragsters entering the scene, and achieving performances on a par with those in California – the heart of VW drag racing and the birthplace of most of the major technical developments.

Even though the Beetle was never conceived as a car in which to burn rubber, Beetles over the years have been tweaked and modified to produce many times their original horsepower, all in search of the lowest time down the quarter-mile, with their rear-mounted engine providing a useful traction advantage when leaving the line.

While many enthusiasts will simply take their street-driven, perhaps mildly-modified, car

down the track at the weekend, a growing number of Beetles have been purpose-built with the express intention of covering a quarter-mile as fast as possible. From turbochargers to nitrous oxide injection, all methods are used to wring every last ounce of power from the humble flat-four. Indeed, in the higher classes, the rules only dictate that the car must have an engine of the "same configuration" as a standard VW, so as long as there's a flat-four under all the ducting and hoses, it's eligible, even if it has a tube-framed chassis and a fiberglass bodyshell.

Such a device is Brian Burrows' "Outrage II," powered by a 2.8-liter, turbocharged, methanol-injected engine, pumping out some 650bhp at the wheels and 512lb ft of torque at 7400rpm. The engine uses mostly U.S.-developed components, including an Autocraft crankcase and cylinder heads, and sits ahead of the driver in a chrome-alloy tube chassis which is covered by a Beetle-shaped fiberglass bodyshell. Power is transmitted to the ground through a Chevrolet Powerglide automatic transmission with a solid Ford rear axle, and the braking system includes twin parachutes.

In August 1993, the car had achieved a record of just 8.12 seconds for the quarter-mile at a terminal speed of 161mph, while in the U.S., speeds of over 170mph from purpose-built dragsters are not uncommon. Brian is hoping to achieve another 70bhp with the addition of nitrous oxide injection, in order to break the eight-second barrier. The speed of 161mph from "Outrage II" represents a U.K. speed record, but the all-time

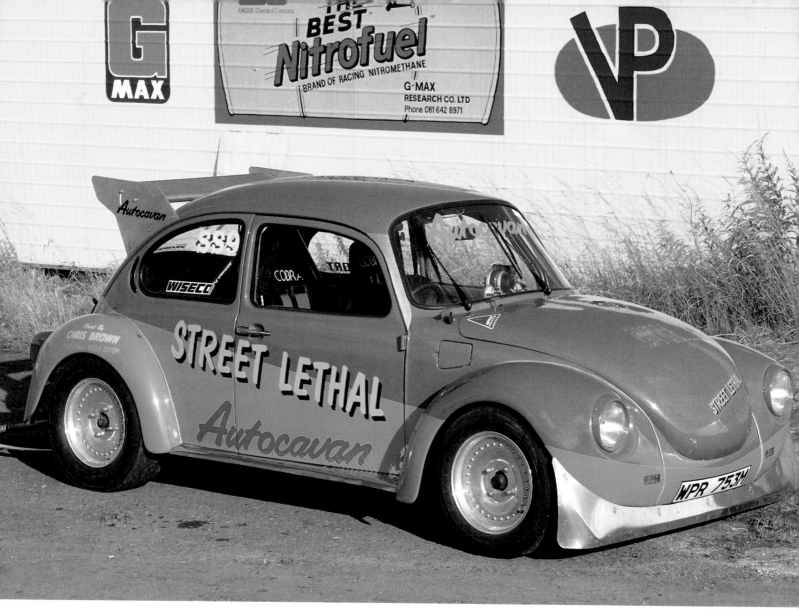

record is currently held by Bernie Smith, with his "rail"-style dragster.

To put these figures in perspective, experts reckon that a Lamborghini Diablo could manage a time of around 15 seconds down the dragstrip, while a state-of-the-art Formula 1 car would probably only manage around 13 or 14 seconds; not bad going for a People's Car! Drag-racing success is not limited to all-out race cars however, with the winners in the street-legal classes achieving times of 10 seconds and speeds of up to 126mph.

The U.K. VWDRC championships include a wide range of different classes. The "Street" Class requires cars to be road-registered and have an MoT, and forbids major modifications such as nitrous oxide injection or turbocharging, although it does not limit the engine size; and "Super Street" adds slick tires, nitrous oxide, turbocharging and racing fuel to the above. In the "Modified" class, anything goes, with the only stipulation being that the car must use a "VW-style" engine, and this class includes vehicles as diverse as "funny cars" and beach buggies. The fourth class caters for kit-cars and beach buggies; it is not at present heavily subscribed, although at least one Fugitive off-road rail has been seen on the strips, making 10-second passes at around 120mph.

Drag-racing is not the only area of motorsport where the Beetle has tasted success: from the earliest days, Beetles have been seen in rallying, autocross and circuit racing, and there is even a championship for Beetle-based single-seater racing cars. The story of the single-seat Beetle racing car began in California (where else?) where a single-seater racing car had been constructed, with a tubular chassis and plastic body, using Beetle mechanical components. The Formcar, as it was called, was raced in privately-organized competitions from around 1963, with the cars restricted to using unmodified Beetle mechanical components.

In 1965, the car was demonstrated to a group which included Porsche's son Ferry, and the Porsche racing manager. They immediately ordered four of the cars and took them back to Germany, to an enthusiastic response. The Porsche firm became the importer for the cars, and a Volkswagen racing formula was introduced, called the Formula Vee. It was an immediate success, providing an accessible and much cheaper form of motorsport than those already available, as the Volkswagen parts were easy and inexpensive to obtain.

The tight restrictions on modifications meant that the costs did not escalate dramatically as the

LEFT: John Brewster's "Street lethal" drag-racing Beetle is fully road-legal, using a full Beetle body and chassis, yet can turn in quarter-mile times of around 10 seconds at 126 mph.

RIGHT: "Europe's fastest VW" – Brian Burrows' "Outrage II" funny car, a record breaker in 1993.

BELOW RIGHT: The 2.8-liter, turbocharged, methanol-injected engine in "Outrage II" pumps out around 700bhp with nitrous-oxide injection, but uses virtually no standard VW components!

BELOW: The grid at the first Formula Vee race, held at the Nurburgring in 1966. The carts used Beetle mechanical parts to provide a low-cost racing formula.

sport took off, and the power outputs of the cars were closely matched, making the races all about driver skill. The Formula quickly spread to other countries, and even produced some pretty talented drivers – Niki Lauda progressed from the humble beginnings of Formula Vee to eventually become a three-times Formula 1 World Champion.

The Formula Vee was effectively superseded in 1971 by the Formula Super Vee, allowing use of the Type 4 engine and double-jointed rear suspension – cars in this new Formula were achieving performances to match Formula 3 cars of the time, and provided a new (if more expensive) route into top-level motorsport. In 1978, the water-cooled engines were permitted in Super Vee. Although both Super Vee and Formula Vee have declined in prominence over the last couple of decades; nowadays it has become a rather obscure branch of motorsport, but with an enthusiastic following nonetheless.

A circuit-racing series for the Beetle has been organized since 1989 in Germany where the nine-round Käfer Cup, including not only circuit racing, but also hillclimbs and slaloms, remains a popular championship. In 1992 the idea was brought to the U.K. with the introduction of the 10-round Beetle Cup series. Organized by Big Boys Toys, an Essex-based engine builder and supplier of custom and tuning parts for the Beetle, the Beetle Cup provides an ideal low-cost entry route to motorsport.

To enter the series, the necessary kit is purchased from the organizers (at about £1600 or $2400), which includes the engine, roll-cage, fire extinguisher, racing seat and fire-retardant clothing, after which all you need is a suitable post-'57 swing-axle Beetle. The engine crankcases are sealed, with the engine being returned to the organizers for any repairs. The 1641cc unit is fitted with an Engle 120° cam, Melling oil pump, "009" centrifugal distributor, and a Dellorto 40mm carburetor. The suspension can be lowered to a minimum ground clearance of 4.7in. (120mm), interior trim and both bumpers are removed, and the minimum weight limit is 1653lb (775kg).

Power outputs from the Beetle Cup cars are around 70bhp at the wheels and top speed is somewhere around the 100mph mark. Although somewhat slower than most other one-make championship series, the Beetle Cup certainly provides some close racing and spectacular action, with the swing-axle suspension, famous for its unforgiving behaviour, providing no shortage of excitement for those pushing the limit. Having driven one of the Cup cars at the Mallory Park circuit, I can report that it certainly feels a lot faster from the inside, with the race-prepared cars proving remarkably composed around the bends compared to their standard counterparts.

Beetles have also been a popular choice for those competing in rallycross events, where again, the traction advantages of the rear-mounted engine were useful. For most competitors, the Beetle has been superseded in this sport by the latest breed of four-wheel supercars, many of them refugees from the outlawed Group B rallying class, such as the Audi Quattro and Ford RS200.

However, Beetle racers don't give up easily, and one man still holding his own against the supercars is Peter Harrold, although it has to be said that his Beetle is more than slightly modified. The car uses a Porsche Carrera five-speed transmission, modified to provide four-wheel drive through a BMW propshaft to front wheels mounted on Golf driveshafts and hubs, with a BMW differential.

The engine had previously been developed to produce around 300bhp, but cylinder-head overheating problems led to the use of water-cooled heads. Not just any heads were used though; a pair of 16-valve heads from the Subaru Legacy were bolted on to the engine, and the camshafts are driven by a belt drive from a modified VW crankshaft. Jawa cylinder liners from a speedboat are used, encased in Porsche barrels, together with Kugelfischer mechanical fuel injection and a Garrett T4 turbocharger. The full power potential of this amazing 16-valve turbo, four-wheel-drive Beetle is said to be around the 500bhp mark – a far cry from those early Porsche prototypes of the 1930s.

BELOW: Beetle Cup car No. 20 is flat out on the straight.

BOTTOM: De Coppen Bros drag car sits next to "Sum Fun."

Index

ACKNOWLEDGMENTS

The author and publisher would like to thank David Eldred, the designer; Stephen Small, the editor and picture researcher; Veronica Price and Nicki Giles, for production; Ron Watson for preparing the index; and the individuals and institutions listed below for supplying the pictures:

Brompton Books, pages: 8, 10-11(bottom), 19(top), 20, 21, 66(Nicky Wright), 67(bottom/Nicky Wright), 77(bottom)
Colin Burnham, pages: 25(bottom), 29(bottom), 30(both), 31(both), 34(top), 35(top), 53(bottom), 59(bottom), 64(bottom), 70(middle), 72(bottom), 73(top), 74(top), 75(top right), 78(bottom)
Fotocompli, pages: 2-3
Mike Key, pages: 1, 4-5,
22-3(all three), 24, 25(top), 26-7, 32-3, 35(bottom), 36-7(all three), 38-9, 40-1(all three), 42-3, 44-5(all three), 47(top), 48-9, 51, 52(both), 53(top), 56(middle & bottom), 57(both), 58(both), 59(top right), 60-1(all three), 62-3(all three), 64(top), 65, 70(bottom), 71(bottom), 72(middle), 73(bottom), 74(bottom), 75(top left), 76(top), 77(top & middle), 78(middle)
Andrew Morland, pages: 14(both), 28(bottom), 29(top left & right), 54-5, 56(top), 67(top), 68-9, 71(top)
Porsche W.G., pages: 6-7, 9
Volkswagen AG, pages: 10-11(top)
Paul Wager, pages: 12-13(all three), 15, 16-17, 18, 19(bottom), 34(bottom), 46(top), 47(bottom), 50